The True Story of
Teeny Tiny Tomi
Even Puppies Have Guardian Angels

Written by
Sue Meller

Illustrated by
Don Collins

Halo
PUBLISHING INTERNATIONAL

Copyright © 2024 Sue Meller. All rights reserved.
Illustrated by Don Collins

No part of this publication may be reproduced, stored in a retrieval system or transmitted in any form or by any means, electronic, mechanical, photocopying, recording or otherwise, without prior permission of Halo Publishing International.

The views and opinions expressed in this book are those of the author and do not necessarily reflect the official policy or position of Halo Publishing International. Any content provided by our authors are of their opinion and are not intended to malign any religion, ethnic group, club, organization, company, individual or anyone or anything.

For permission requests, write to the publisher, addressed "Attention: Permissions Coordinator," at the address below.

Halo Publishing International
7550 W IH-10 #800, PMB 2069,
San Antonio, TX 78229

First Edition, November 2024
ISBN: 978-1-63765-669-3
Library of Congress Control Number: 2024917349

Halo Publishing International is a self-publishing company that publishes adult fiction and non-fiction, children's literature, self-help, spiritual, and faith-based books. Do you have a book idea you would like us to consider publishing? Please visit www.halopublishing.com for more information.

Chapter 1
Teeny Tiny Tomi's Lucky Day

An adorable black puppy, whose eyes were not yet open, was left in a box by the bus stop. She was tiny and had no momma, no brothers or sisters. However, she was not really alone. She had guardian angels watching over her. At first, these were guardian angels looking after her from heaven. Eventually, her earthbound guardian angels began to appear.

Guardian angels are kind, caring people or nurturing animals. They guide and help. This puppy's special angels would change her life forever.

The first guardian angel was a homeless man who found the puppy and picked her up, hoping to save her life. He did not have much to give except human kindness. He comforted her by holding her close to his chest.

The man knew babies need milk, so he went to the store and bought PET Evaporated Milk because he thought it was food for puppies. The man gently took his new friend to a shady spot where he opened the can of milk and put some drops on his fingers. He tried to feed the puppy by putting those drops on her lips.

Then, along came the puppy's second guardian angel—a lady named Sue who was going into a store. She saw the man holding the puppy. Sue went over to speak with him and offered to care for the little one. He said no; he wanted to do it because the puppy was his new special friend.

When Sue came out of the store, she asked where the man lived. He said he lived on the streets. That is how he knew the little puppy needed his help. He understood what it meant not to have a home or a family or friends to care about him.

"Why are you homeless?" Sue asked.

He truthfully said, "I'm a bad alcoholic."

Knowing that alcoholism is a horrible disease, Sue inquired if he needed help for himself.

He politely answered, "No, ma'am, I'm too far gone."

Sue again offered to take the puppy.

Somehow, deep down in his heart, the man knew he could not care for his new little friend, so he agreed to give Sue the puppy if she paid him one hundred dollars.

After going to a bank, Sue handed the man the one hundred dollars he requested. She hoped he would use it to buy himself some good food and not just more beer.

With tears streaming down his face, the man tenderly gave the pup a kiss on her head and reluctantly placed her in Sue's hands.

As she walked toward her car, the man came over to Sue and asked if he could kiss the puppy goodbye one more time. "Yes, of course. What is your name?" she asked him.

He answered, "Tommy."

Sue said, "Well, why don't we name the puppy after you?"

The man said we could not do that because it was a girl puppy, and Tommy was a boy's name.

"If we change the spelling to *T-O-M-I*, then it would be a girl's name," she said.

Tommy threw his hands up in the air and got a big smile on his face. He leaned over and gave the puppy another soft kiss on her head.

Sue then named the puppy Teeny Tiny Tomi, put her on her lap, and drove directly to a veterinarian for a checkup.

Great News!

The veterinarian looked Teeny Tiny Tomi over and said she was in good health. She also said she thought the puppy was only about a week old.

Goodness, now I have a puppy to take care of! Sue thought to herself.

The veterinarian said that Teeny Tiny Tomi immediately needed puppy formula to provide nourishment since there was no momma dog. In addition, it would be helpful to find a momma dog willing to feed Teeny Tiny Tomi and let her play with other newborn puppies.

Author's note:

Following each chapter there will be a box of discussion topics. I hope you will take time to think about these and talk about them with your friends and family.

❖ Life's Challenges
- Abandoned animals
- Homelessness
- Addiction
- Choice to spend $100 on the puppy instead of a new blouse

❖ Lessons Of Compassion
- Homeless man's rescue of a puppy and his empathy
- Importance of animals to the homeless
- Offering of help to both the puppy and the homeless alcoholic man

Chapter 2
Teeny Tiny Tomi Meets the Neighbors and More Guardian Angels

To take care of her, Sue took Teeny Tiny Tomi home. Her neighbors came over as soon as they heard about the baby pup. Now, Teeny Tiny Tomi had new guardian angels who wanted to help in their own special ways.

Sue's neighbor Deanna went shopping just as you would for a human baby. She bought puppy formula, baby bottles, a hot-water bottle to make Teeny Tiny Tomi feel as if she were next to her own momma, a really soft blanket with hearts and puppies on it, and a toy with which to snuggle. Teeny Tiny Tomi was all set.

Teeny Tiny Tomi's next guardian angel was a twelve-year-old girl named Ava. She gave the little one lots of sweet hugs and fed her a bottle of the special formula.

The internet has a wealth of information on how to care for a baby puppy. A great tip: If you put a hoodie on backwards, you can put the puppy in the hood and cuddle it close to your chest.

This made it easy for Sue to take Teeny Tiny Tomi on walks around the neighborhood while carefully tucked into her bright-yellow hoody. Everyone she met along the way wanted to know the story of Teeny Tiny Tomi.

❖ Life's Challenges
- Caring for an abandoned puppy

❖ Lessons Of Compassion
- Teamwork: Neighbors coming together without being asked

Chapter 3
More Angels, More Friends, and Learning a Very Important Lesson

Sue had lots of questions about caring for such a small puppy.

Momma dogs help puppies go to the bathroom by licking them. No problem—warm cotton pads worked just fine. Teeny Tiny Tomi was soon tinkling like crazy, but she just would not poop.

So one of Teeny Tiny Tomi's guardian angels, Deanna, watched a video on how to get a baby puppy to poop. She massaged the puppy for about half an hour and...success! Teeny Tiny Tomi's guardian angel in charge of pooping had come to the rescue. This is super important because pooping is the body's way of getting rid of waste in both puppies and humans, thus keeping them healthy.

From the time they are born, puppies ideally should be with other puppies so they can develop socialization skills. This is necessary so that they grow up to be good friends of both people and other animals. Another guardian angel came along with a terrific idea.

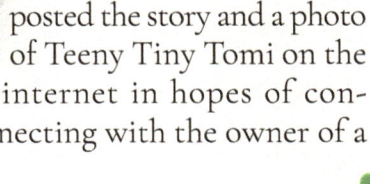

Sue's best friend, Ann, posted the story and a photo of Teeny Tiny Tomi on the internet in hopes of connecting with the owner of a new-momma dog. The posting was seen by someone who knew someone, who knew someone, who would be Teeny Tiny Tomi's next guardian angel, a retired veterinarian named Jan. She was the owner of Lucy, a beautiful golden retriever that had recently had a litter of puppies.

But would Lucy and her puppies accept Teeny Tiny Tomi?

Sue, Ann, and Jan talked on the phone and set up a meeting in a park. Nine of the cutest black golden-doodle puppies and Lucy awaited Teeny Tiny Tomi's arrival.

Lucy welcomed Teeny Tiny Tomi and was glad to lend an extra teat to another hungry puppy. With a little sniff and a lick or two, she nudged Teeny Tiny Tomi closer and began feeding her with the other puppies.

Teeny Tiny Tomi knew just what to do. She latched on quickly. She had no idea where her angel momma had come from, but was so glad to have her milk. From that moment on, Teeny Tiny Tomi became a member of Lucy's family and never again had to worry about having a home or food.

A very fortunate Teeny Tiny Tomi now had eleven more guardian angels: Jan, Lucy, and Lucy's nine doodle puppies. They all joined together to love and care for her. Because Teeny Tiny Tomi was black, like all the doodles, Jan gave her a bright-orange collar so she would stand out from the other puppies. Then, off she went on a new adventure, her eyes having just opened and weighing only one and a half pounds.

❖ Life's Challenges

- Socialization of both animals and humans
- Finding a home and nurturing family
- Adoption

❖ Lessons Of Compassion

- Lending a teat or other life-sustaining assistance
- Acceptance/adoption by both Lucy and Jan
- Creating a loving home

Chapter 4
Off to the Ranch

Jan and her family had a home in the city, as well as a ranch and a horse farm. That meant there were lots of new guardian angels for Teeny Tiny Tomi to get to know, including Jan's husband, Steve, their five children, and lots of animals. There were horses, a calf named August, a cat, and an assortment of other dogs.

The ten adorable puppies ate and grew, ate and grew, and ate and grew. Pretty soon, the pack of pups, their small eyes just having opened, began to explore their home and yard. At first, it was slow, a sniff here and a sniff there. That quickly advanced to running and scattered games of tag. Sometimes, the puppies raced in circles around the fig tree and yanked its leaves. This was a source of endless entertainment for the puppy family.

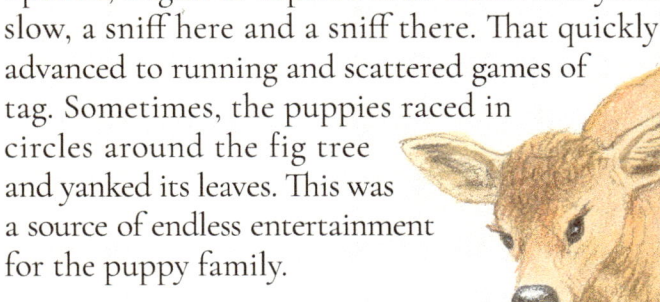

Teeny Tiny Tomi grew by leaps and bounds; her belly became plump, her legs bowed out, and her tail curled up. She started to look quite different from her siblings who had soft, silky hair in waves all over their bodies. Teeny Tiny Tomi's short locks were wiry and coarse, in tufts and fringe here and there. She looked like a street dog, a ruffian, but her looks really did not matter.

All the golden-doodle puppies loved to play with Teeny Tiny Tomi and give her orange collar a tug. She played and wrestled with any and all of them. She even pounced on the cat. Her fiery personality and her sweet disposition were coming to life.

The golden doodles had a purebred golden-retriever momma and a purebred black-poodle daddy. But who exactly were Teeny Tiny Tomi's ancestors?

Being a veterinarian, Jan was able to send some of Teeny Tiny Tomi's blood to a laboratory for DNA testing. She was quite the mixture:

Guard
32% American Staffordshire Terrier
25% American Pit Bull Terrier
12% Doberman Pinscher
7% American Bulldog
3% Boxer
3% Rottweiler
2% Bullmastiff
1% Boston Terrir

Terrier
2% Chihuahua

Companion
5% Shih Tzu
2% Lhasa Apso

Asian and Oceanian
3% Chinese Shar-Pei

Sporting
3% Cocker Spaniel

WOW! DEFINITELY ONE OF A KIND!

❀ Life's Challenges

- Looking and being different
- Learning how to play with others
- Accepting and being accepted, no matter your pedigree

❀ Lessons Of Compassion

- The doodle puppies did not care what Tomi looked like. They played with her and loved her anyway.

Chapter 5
Learning Some Rules and Going to College

Soon, Teeny Tiny Tomi was six months old but still a puppy—playful and a bit crazy. However, she was no longer teeny tiny. So, going forward, she was just called Tomi. It was time to start teaching Tomi the basics of becoming a good dog.

She slowly became housebroken; she slept almost all the way through the night, sat on command, and waited until food was put in front of her. Tomi was also a free spirit who loved the outdoors and getting into cow manure or anything else smelly and fun. She just was not at all interested in walking on a leash.

Jan was placing the golden-doodle puppies with their "forever" families. She also had many other responsibilities: taking care of the ranch and horse farm, cattle, numerous dogs, that cat, and, most importantly, her family. She just was not sure she could keep Tomi forever. She knew better than anyone that puppies needed a lot of attention and training. The problem was that Jan and her family had grown extremely fond of Tomi, and they just could not see adopting her out to someone they did not know.

What to do?

What to do?

Jan and Sue talked and talked. Sue would, of course, take Tomi back, but was worried she would be lonely. Sue did not have any other animals for Tomi to play with, and she was often away from home.

Jan came up with a perfect solution. Tomi and her son's dog, Whitney, a little imp, had become besties. They wrestled and played and were a good matched pair. But Jan's son, Zach—Tomi's next guardian angel—was returning to college at Texas Tech University in Lubbock and taking Whitney with him, so each dog was losing its bestie. Then, Jan and Zach came up with a great idea—Tomi would go to college too!

Tomi climbed into Zach's truck, and off they all went.

Zach lived with several roommates. They had a nice big house with a fenced yard and a dog door for zooming in and out. Between running and chasing, and running and chasing, Whitney and Tomi went with Zach to his work at the Lamesa Veterinary Clinic and learned about all sorts of other farm animals.

However, this was not just going to be all fun and games. Every day, Tomi and Whitney went to puppy-training classes and learned how to be good pets and interact with the outside world.

Tomi and Whitney

🐾 Life's Challenges
- Obedience
- Learning to live in a community
- Going to school
- Responsibilities

🐾 Lessons Of Compassion
- Empathy
- Loving forever adoption
- What it means to be a friend

Epilogue

For nine months, Teeny Tiny Tomi had been watched over by a team of guardian angels. Soon, she was able to turn all that care and love into a future in which she would earn her own guardian angel wings.

The Real Teeny Tiny Tomi

How One Act of Kindness at a Time Changed Teeny Tiny Tomi's World

A Lesson for Us All

The story of Teeny Tiny Tomi has many lessons.

The most important is a reminder that every life is precious and deserving of our concern and our kindness.

You will never know what changes you can make until you begin extending a helping hand, just as Teeny Tiny Tomi's guardian angels did for her.

❖ Guardian Angels
- Help you to help yourself
- Help you to help others
- Show empathy
- Show kindness
- Are ever present

Acknowledgments

As with any project, MANY WONDERFUL PEOPLE had a part in this story. I would first like to acknowledge three of those very important people.

Without the original Tommy, this book would not have happened. His sweetness and empathy were the catalysts for the story and for the closer examination by all of us of the nature of homelessness and addiction. His heart and soul were on display in the most touching and profound ways.

Jan Roush Held is a Texas A&M graduate in veterinary medicine. She and her family showed us what hard work, compassion, and a huge heart can produce. Jan has continuously poured her many talents and time into caring for all animals, large and small. She and her family live on a ranch in Liberty Hill, Texas. Her son, Zach, is Tomi's forever family.

Don Collins was a University of Texas graduate. He had a long career as a commercial illustrator. The illustrations he produced for this book brilliantly capture the spirit of Teeny Tiny Tomi and all her guardian angels. We are sad that he passed away before seeing his work in print.

In addition, there were these guardian angels: Ava Stewart, Deanna King, Ann Kilby, Jan Roush Held, Lucy and her goldendoodle puppies, Steve Held, and Zach Roush.

Also, along the way, many people gave their time, talents, and insights. They read and reread, edited, suggested changes, and gave support. These included: Mike Levy, Kathy Caskey, Toni Schmid Stevenson, Ann Kilby, Kathleen Niendorff, Rose Betty Williams, Mary Chalmers, Dwain Kelley, Cliff Ernst, Trish Wilson, and Alan Graham.

Milton Keynes UK
Ingram Content Group UK Ltd.
UKHW020656131124
451151UK00019B/376